RSYA

SEP 2007

D1266439

Homeland Security and
Counterterrorism Careers

Search and Rescue Specialist

and Careers in FEMA

by Monica Ferry

Enslow Publishers, Inc.
40 Industrial Road
Box 398
Berkeley Heights, NJ 07922
USA

http://www.enslow.com

Library of Congress Cataloging-in-Publication Data

Ferry, Monica.
  Search and rescue specialist and careers in FEMA / Monica Ferry.
     p. cm. — (Homeland security and counterterrorism careers)
  Includes bibliographical references and index.
  ISBN 0-7660-2650-7
  1. United States. Federal Emergency Management Agency—Vocational guidance—Juvenile literature. 2. Rescue work—United States—Juvenile literature. 3. Search and rescue operations—United States—Juvenile literature. 4. Emergency management—United States—Juvenile literature. I. Title. II. Series.
  HV551.3.F47 2006
  363.34023'73—dc22
                                        2006015850

Printed in the United States of America

10 9 8 7 6 5 4 3 2 1

To Our Readers:
We have done our best to make sure all Internet Addresses in this book were active and appropriate when we went to press. However, the author and the publisher have no control over and assume no liability for the material available on those Internet sites or on other Web sites they may link to. Any comments or suggestions can be sent by e-mail to comments@enslow.com or to the address on the back cover.

Photo Credits: Associated Press, Anchorage Daily News, p. 97; Associated Press, AP, pp. 20, 46–47, 51, 58, 100; Associated Press, The Charlotte Observer, p. 96; Photo courtesy of the Exxon Valdez Oil Spill Trustee Council, p. 38; FEMA, pp. 1, 4, 5, 7, 9, 10–11, 13, 15, 17, 18, 19, 24, 25 (adapted from diagram by FEMA), 28, 29, 31, 32 (adapted from diagram by FEMA), 36, 40, 42, 43, 49, 53, 54, 56, 62, 65, 67, 69, 71, 72, 73, 77, 78, 79, 80, 83, 85, 86, 90, 91, 92, 94, 95, 99, 102, 103, 107, 108, 109, 111, 112, 114, 115, 116, 117, 118, 119, 120, 121, 122, 123, 124, 125, 126, 127, 128; Getty Images/Stone, p. 61; Library of Congress, p. 39; U.S. Customs and Border Protection, James R. Tourtellotte, pp. 21, 23.

Cover Photo: FEMA, Corbis/Royalty-Free (background)

Contents

On September 11, 2001, disaster response workers did all they could to save people at the World Trade Center. Many of them sacrificed their own lives.

Chapter 1

September 11, 2001

On September 11, 2001, life in the United States changed forever. Terrorists hijacked four planes. Two of the planes crashed into the twin towers of the World Trade Center in New York City. A third struck the Pentagon in Washington, D.C. Thousands of innocent people died. A fourth airplane in Pennsylvania was part of the same terrorist attack. It crashed into a field, killing many more people. All of this happened in just a few short hours.

The first plane hit the North Tower of the World Trade Center at about 8:45 in the morning. It set the building on fire and left a massive hole in the tower's side.[1] Within minutes, first responders jumped into action. These emergency workers included firefighters, police officers, paramedics, and others. People who worked at the Trade Center rushed down stairways to escape the building. At the same time, the emergency workers climbed those same stairs toward the scene of the disaster. They were doing their job. Some helped survivors out of the building. Others put out the fires. Still others rescued the injured.

Everything happened quickly. A second plane crashed into the South Tower of the Trade Center just after 9:00 A.M. The government closed all airports in the New York City area. Bridges and tunnels around the city were closed as well. Within the hour, every airport in the country had been closed. Never before in the nation's history had this happened. Airplanes were ordered to land at once. Only military and government airplanes would fly during the next few days. By 9:45 that morning, a third plane had struck the Pentagon.

Life in the United States came to a standstill. The military went on high alert. Special plans went into effect to protect President George W. Bush. He was visiting a school in Sarasota, Florida. By 10:00 A.M., he was on his way to an Air Force base in Louisiana. Security workers rushed Vice President Dick Cheney to a safe place away from the White House. They feared that the White House might be attacked, too.

Hundreds of police, firefighters, and rescue workers were sent to the World Trade Center and the Pentagon.

FEMA employees worked around the clock to
clear debris after the 9/11 attacks.

Their actions were heroic, but more than three thousand people lost their lives. It was the greatest man-made disaster in U.S. history. Among the dead were 343 New York City firefighters. Sixty officers from the New York City Police and Port Authority died as well.[2] All these men and women lost their lives trying to save others.

How would the nation respond? What would happen next? At 1:00 P.M., President Bush spoke to the nation. He assured Americans that security efforts were

---

It was the greatest man-made disaster in U.S. history. Among the dead were 343 New York City firefighters and sixty officers from the New York City Police and Port Authority.

---

in place. He said the U.S. military was on high alert around the globe. He asked Americans to pray for those killed or hurt in the attack. "The search is underway for those who are behind these evil acts," he reassured the country. "I've directed the full resources of our intelligence and law enforcement communities to find those responsible and to bring them to justice."[3] Fighting terrorism would become the nation's number-one priority in the following years.

Man-made and Natural Disasters

A disaster is man-made if humans cause it to happen. The terrorist attacks of September 11, 2001, were a man-made disaster. A natural disaster is caused by nature and is usually out of our control. Hurricane Katrina is an example of a natural disaster. This hurricane struck the Gulf Coast in August 2005. It left most of New Orleans, Louisiana, underwater (below). It also destroyed cities and towns along the coast of Mississippi. FEMA is the part of the U.S. government that helps people following both man-made and natural disasters.

FEMA created the National Urban Search and Rescue (US&R) Response System in 1989.[4] The goal was to bring together specialists from emergency services into teams that can respond to disasters. These teams include people from fire departments, law enforcement, government agencies, and private companies. When a disaster occurs, FEMA sends its teams to respond.

What is search and rescue? This is the action that takes place whenever a person is missing and may need medical attention. For example, a small child might wander away from home and get stuck in a dangerous place. Someone might get lost in the wilderness while hiking. Another person might fall off a boat and need to be found and rescued from the water.

Urban search and rescue takes place in urban areas like cities and towns. It involves people who have become trapped after a disaster. First, US&R team members help to find these people in the rubble of a building. Then they provide medical treatment until victims can be taken to a hospital.

US&R teams respond to many types of disasters. These include earthquakes, hurricanes, severe storms and tornadoes, floods, mining accidents, transportation accidents, and terrorist attacks. The emergency might happen slowly, like a hurricane. It might also happen quickly and without notice, like an explosion or an earthquake.

FEMA manages twenty-eight US&R teams. The teams are located around the country. Sixty-two people work on each team. Each task force has more than 130 members to make sure a full team can respond at a moment's notice.[5]

People came from all over the United States to help with rescue and cleanup after September 11, also called 9/11. The Federal Emergency Management Agency (FEMA) is part of the U.S. government. It responds to emergencies. It also manages other groups that provide help after a disaster. On 9/11, FEMA sent twelve Urban Search and Rescue (US&R) teams to search for victims in the rubble of the buildings. Eight teams went to New York, and four teams went to Washington, D.C. That number soon grew. In all, twenty teams worked in New York City and five in Washington.[6]

FEMA's US&R teams are trained to respond when a building collapses. This is what happened at the World Trade Center and the Pentagon very soon after the airplanes struck. Each US&R team includes local emergency workers—firefighters, emergency medical workers, and doctors. Engineers and other experts are also part of the teams. Specially trained search dogs with their handlers are on US&R teams, too. After the 9/11 terrorist attacks, FEMA teams worked around the clock. At first their job was to find survivors in the rubble. Sadly, very few were found. Identifying the remains of the dead was the main task at hand.

So much needed to be done in New York City. For one thing, it took several weeks to put out the fires at the site of the former World Trade Center. The site had to be cleaned up, and the debris had to be taken away. This job would take many months. Not until May 2002 did the last truckload of rubble leave Ground Zero, as

One of the main tasks after 9/11 was to find missing people. This FEMA employee looks at a wall of pictures showing people who were still missing after the attacks.

the site became known. By then, 1.8 million tons of material had been removed from the site.[7]

Much more had to be done. Missing people had to be located. Survivors needed food, shelter, and counseling. The families of those who had died needed help, too. Thousands of volunteers helped at Ground Zero and around the city. These people, too, had to be fed and cared for. Organizations such as the Red Cross and the Salvation Army offered assistance. FEMA helped to coordinate the efforts of all these groups.

FEMA also opened the Disaster Assistance Service Center in New York City. The center was open for several years after 9/11. FEMA's individual assistance officers staffed the center. They worked with thousands of victims of the disaster.

What did the officers do? For one thing, about fifty thousand people had worked at the World Trade Center on any given day.[8] After 9/11, these people no longer had a place to work. Many of them lost their jobs. FEMA gave Trade Center employees money from the government to pay their bills. The agency helped them until they could find new work.

Many people lost their homes after the disaster because they could no longer pay the rent. FEMA helped these people find a new place to live and pay their rent. People from all over the world come to live in New York City. Many do not speak English. FEMA hired translators in more than thirty-five languages. They worked at the service center to help 9/11 victims and their families.

In the days after the disaster, FEMA sent dozens of disaster assistance employees to New York. They walked the streets of downtown Manhattan handing out fliers. The fliers provided information in many languages. They told people where to find help. The FEMA workers made sure everyone who needed help knew where to find it.

The emotional effects of disasters are long lasting. FEMA's community relations specialists counseled survivors and families of 9/11 victims. FEMA provided funding for other counselors to help in these efforts.

Search and Rescue Specialist

After 9/11, FEMA quickly set up the Disaster Assistance Service Center in New York City. The center's staff gave victims information about where to find help.

These counselors worked in both New York City and Washington, D.C. Their work continued for months.

The 9/11 terrorist attacks took the United States by surprise. Afterward, the country united to deal with the tragedy. Thousands of people took part in the rescue and cleanup work. The staff of FEMA coordinated the workers during the recovery.

Disasters such as 9/11 show just how important FEMA is to the nation's safety. FEMA trains its workers to be ready for disasters. It responds to natural disasters such as Hurricanes Katrina and Rita in 2005. It also responds to man-made disasters such as 9/11.

The United States learned from 9/11. Today the country has laws that help uncover terrorist activities.

FEMA responds to natural disasters such as Hurricanes Katrina and Rita in 2005. It also responds to man-made disasters such as 9/11.

The Department of Homeland Security (DHS) was created in 2002 to protect the nation. Thousands of people work for the department. Some keep track of terrorists and try to predict their next move. Others warn Americans when there is a risk of an attack. This allows people to be better prepared.

FEMA is part of the DHS. FEMA plans to make the emergency-response workers of the United States better prepared than ever. Its workers are ready to deal with disasters of any kind. Sometimes disasters cannot be prevented, however. That is when FEMA is needed the most. This book takes a closer look at the people who work for FEMA. It also looks at careers in emergency management.

An Urban Search and Rescue team member searches a home for survivors after Hurricane Katrina in 2005.

FEMA is one of twenty-two government agencies brought together into the Department of Homeland Security (DHS).

Chapter 2

Inside FEMA

After 9/11, U.S. leaders decided to make changes in the way the government worked. They wanted the nation to work harder to prevent terrorist attacks. They also wanted to be better prepared if they did happen. Working with Congress, President Bush created the Department of Homeland Security (DHS) in 2002. The DHS brought together twenty-two agencies. One of them was FEMA. By 2005, the DHS had almost 180,000 employees.[1] They work in offices all over the United States.

The DHS has three main goals:

- to prevent terrorist attacks within the United States
- to reduce America's vulnerability to terrorism
- to minimize damage from attacks and natural disasters[2]

Before the DHS was created, its agencies worked alone. They did not always share information. They

President Bush signs the law creating the DHS on November 25, 2002. He is surrounded by members of Congress.

did not work together to solve problems. U.S. leaders believed that these agencies would work better if they cooperated. The September 11 attacks had made this clear.

What Does the DHS Do?

The focus of the DHS is to protect the American people and homeland. Its job is to spot threats to the country. This includes both natural and man-made disasters. It works to prevent threats from becoming reality. When disasters do occur, the DHS must respond quickly.

Search and Rescue Specialist

The DHS has many responsibilities. Different parts of the department handle each one. Some DHS employees look for weak spots in the country's infrastructure—the systems that keep the country running. Infrastructure includes transportation (roads, airports, and bridges) and communication systems

In December 2002, former DHS leader Tom Ridge speaks to U.S. Customs employees about their transition to the new department.

(telephones, computers, and the Internet). Other DHS staff members collect data, or information. They use it to see what problems exist and what problems could come up in the future. Then they work with communities and companies to solve problems or to keep them from happening.

Here are a few examples of what DHS agencies do[3]:

- U.S. Customs and Border Protection watches U.S. borders. It tries to prevent terrorists and their weapons from entering the United States. It also tries to make sure that honest trade and travelers can cross the borders with ease.
- The Transportation Security Administration protects the nation's transportation systems. It also tries to make sure people can trade goods freely.
- Many employees of Immigration and Customs Enforcement are investigators. They work to uncover weaknesses at the nation's borders and within transportation systems.
- The Federal Law Enforcement Training Center provides training to law enforcement professionals. This helps them do their jobs better.
- Citizenship and Immigration Services makes sure people follow laws related to immigrating to the United States or becoming a U.S. citizen.
- The U.S. Coast Guard protects the nation's ports and waterways. It also works in international waters to ensure national security.

U.S. Customs and Border Protection keeps the nation's borders secure. These shipping containers are being inspected as they arrive in the United States.

• The U.S. Secret Service protects the president and other high-level officials. It also investigates crime, such as computer-based attacks on the nation.

The Federal Emergency Management Agency

FEMA's motto is "A Nation Prepared." After 9/11, being prepared became more important than ever.

Local and state governments usually share the job of protecting their citizens from disasters. It is also their job to help people recover from them. Sometimes a disaster is so big that they cannot handle it alone. When this happens, a state's governor asks the president for help. The president then officially declares the region a disaster area. At that point, federal assistance is sent. FEMA is the government agency in charge of this effort. Its workers are called in as soon as the president officially declares a disaster.

FEMA's headquarters are located in Washington, D.C. The agency has around 2,600 full-time employees. Some of them work at headquarters. Others work in

FEMA headquarters building in Washington, D.C.

Search and Rescue Specialist

FEMA's Regional Offices

FEMA has ten regional offices located around the country. This map shows each region and the city where the office is located. Each region serves several states. The staff in each office works directly with the states to plan for disasters, develop programs, and respond when major disasters occur.

regional offices located in cities around the country. Still others work in the Mount Weather Emergency Operations Center in Virginia or at the National Emergency Training Center in Maryland.

FEMA also employs nearly four thousand part-time workers. These people are called disaster assistance employees (DAEs). These workers are on standby. They go to work only when a disaster has occurred and FEMA has been called in to help. Then the DAEs travel to the disaster area. They may stay there for weeks or even months to help a community recover.

How FEMA Began

In 1803, a series of terrible fires struck Portsmouth, New Hampshire. The town struggled to recover. It needed money badly. Finally, the citizens turned to the federal government. Congress passed several laws to help the people of Portsmouth. It was the first time the federal government stepped in to help a community during a local emergency. Over the next century, Congress passed more than a hundred laws to help with disaster recovery.[4]

In the twentieth century, the government continued to offer help whenever disasters struck. It provided aid to victims of floods, fires, and other disasters. By the 1970s, more than a hundred agencies took part in the federal response to emergencies. This may seem like a good thing. Sometimes, though, all the agencies made it more difficult to get the job done. Too many people were trying to do the same things. .

State leaders did not want to deal with so many government agencies after a disaster. What if a single agency took charge of federal recovery work? Perhaps that would make all agencies more effective. The states asked President Jimmy Carter to create a new government agency. It would work with communities once a president declared a disaster. It also would organize the work being done by all the different government agencies. President Carter created FEMA in 1979.

FEMA began responding to disasters right away. The agency had a busy year in 1980. Dangerous chemicals were dumped at Love Canal in New York

---

The agency had a busy year in 1980. Dangerous chemicals were dumped at Love Canal in New York State. Mount St. Helens, a volcano in Washington State, erupted. Forest fires struck California, Colorado, and Wisconsin.

State. Mount St. Helens, a volcano in Washington State, erupted. Forest fires struck California, Colorado, and Wisconsin. Severe storms and flooding affected states all over the country. There were tornadoes, typhoons, and hurricanes. New Jersey had a water shortage. Hawaii experienced dangerously high surf. FEMA responded to all of these events.[5]

FEMA provides aid in times of drought or flood. It also sends help when weather hurts farming and fishing interests. One year unusually cold weather killed shrimp

Disaster Facts

Here are a few interesting facts about disasters from FEMA's Web site[6]:

Floods
- Flooding is the most common natural disaster in the United States.
- A grown person can be knocked off his or her feet by rapidly moving floodwaters as shallow as six inches deep.
- Floodwater is almost always contaminated and undrinkable.

Hurricanes
- Hurricanes are tropical storms with sustained winds over 74 miles per hour.
- Hurricane season in the Atlantic Ocean lasts from June 1 through November 30.

Tornadoes

- Tornado winds can reach 300 miles per hour.
- Tornadoes happen most frequently in Tornado Alley. This is a group of states in the middle of the country. It includes Kansas, Oklahoma, and Texas. Tornadoes can occur in other states as well.[7]
- The United States generally sees the most tornado activity between March and August.
- Tornado winds can pick up objects and deposit them more than 100 miles away.
- Most tornadoes last less than ten minutes.

off the coast of Georgia. Many people depended on shrimping to earn a living. FEMA sent money to help these people. In 1994, a weather pattern called El Niño warmed water in the Pacific Northwest. This killed the salmon, a fish that thrives only in cooler temperatures. Citizens in California, Washington, and Oregon received help from FEMA. Their livelihood depended on the salmon, and they needed help to cope with the disaster.

September 11, 2001, changed the whole picture for FEMA. After that, the agency began to focus on being ready to go to work if terrorists should strike again. It needed to help the nation be better prepared to deal with such an attack. As part of the DHS, FEMA worked to help communities face the threat of terrorism.

FEMA employees have the nation's interest at heart, but sometimes their job is difficult and unpredictable. For example, the agency was not prepared when Hurricane Katrina struck the Gulf Coast in August 2005. Many Americans thought that the agency became too focused on terrorism after joining the DHS. As a result, FEMA could no longer respond effectively to a large natural disaster like Hurricane Katrina.

Today, FEMA is constantly working to find the perfect balance. In the future, it hopes to do a better job managing all emergencies—both man-made and natural.

At the National Emergency Training Center, FEMA teaches disaster workers how to respond to emergencies.

What Does FEMA Do?

FEMA's job is to be prepared for the entire "life cycle" of disasters. That is, what happens before, during, and after an emergency? The disaster life cycle describes how emergency workers do the following:

- prepare for emergencies and disasters
- respond to disasters when they occur
- help people and places recover from disasters
- mitigate (lessen) the effects of disasters
- reduce the risk of loss from future disasters
- prevent disasters from occurring[8]

How this works is shown in the chart below. FEMA is involved at every stage of this cycle.

Search and Rescue Specialist

We have learned a lot about FEMA's many responsibilities. We have learned what the agency does before, during, and after a disaster. Here are a few things that are not FEMA's responsibility.

FEMA does <u>not</u>

- **physically rescue people or serve as first responders in a disaster.** This is the responsibility of local and state police, firefighters, and emergency personnel.
- **build dams and levees or activate sand-bagging activities during a flood.** This is usually the responsibility of local and state officials and the U.S. Army Corps of Engineers.
- **take charge of a recovery effort.** FEMA works jointly with state and local officials to manage the effort.
- **run temporary shelters or disaster food stations.** This is usually done by organizations such as the American Red Cross or the Salvation Army.
- **make weather predictions, fly into hurricanes, or predict when rivers will flood.** These activities are the responsibility of the National Weather Service.
- **order evacuations of communities because of a natural disaster.** This is usually the responsibility of state and local officials, but FEMA will help in the effort.
- **set building standards and fire codes.** This is the responsibility of local and state officials, with suggestions from FEMA.
- **call out the National Guard.** This is generally a state responsibility.[9]

Prepare for Emergencies and Disasters

FEMA prepares emergency workers across the country to handle disasters of all types. It provides money and training programs. It also develops plans for how the nation should take action after a disaster. Training exercises are an important part of this task. During these exercises, emergency workers practice how to react to a disaster. They learn how to handle it better

> FEMA prepares emergency workers across the country to handle disasters of all types. It also develops plans for how the nation should take action after a disaster.

and faster. These exercises get the nation's emergency workers ready for a real disaster. Communities all around the country take part in these exercises. They are organized by FEMA employees.

Respond to Disasters When They Occur

First responders must act immediately when a disaster strikes. Thousands of these workers are stationed around the country in every city, town, and village. FEMA helps to make sure they are prepared. The agency also makes sure first responders have the equipment needed to do their jobs. First responders in the United States are among the best in the world. They regularly save lives on the job.

How does FEMA respond to a major disaster? First the president officially declares a disaster. Then FEMA recommends one person to act as the federal coordinating officer (FCO). A disaster may affect more than one state. If so, a different FCO is named for each state. An FCO may be a FEMA staff member. He or she also may be a local or state emergency manager. As a first step, the FCO and the state response team set up a disaster field office. This office is located near the disaster area. Federal and state employees work together from this office. They carry out response and recovery work.

Help People and Places Recover from Disasters

Imagine that the president has declared a disaster. It is time for FEMA to call its disaster assistance employees (DAEs) to action. These workers travel to the disaster area and stay as long as necessary to help the community. They may help people find temporary housing or food. They make sure people have the medication they need. They help victims fill out paperwork so they can receive money from the government. DAEs are asked to do what is needed

This man left his home for Texas when Hurricane Katrina struck. A disaster assistance employee (DAE) is registering him for services.

to return people's lives to normal. For some people, life after a disaster may never be the same. FEMA and other agencies try to help people get on their feet again.

Other FEMA employees work with local and state officials. Perhaps the disaster has damaged public areas, roads, and bridges. FEMA staff work to see that they are rebuilt. These are just some of the ways that FEMA helps people recover from disasters.

Mitigate the Effects of Disasters

Many of FEMA's programs mitigate the effects of disaster. Mitigation is the effort to lessen the effect a disaster has on people's lives. FEMA does this through damage prevention and programs such as the National Flood Insurance Program. FEMA tries to prevent damage from flooding by helping people choose a safe place to build a home. It removes homes from a floodplain area if necessary. FEMA helps to design buildings that can survive earthquakes or terrorist attacks. These activities lessen the effect a disaster can have on a community.

Reduce the Risk of Loss from Future Disasters

The U.S. government has learned from previous disasters. Today it works to reduce the risk for future disasters in many ways. For example, it creates better building and fire codes. These prevent people from building unsafe

Man-made Disasters[10]

Below are some of the deadliest man-made disasters in U.S. history.

May 31, 1889, Johnstown, Pennsylvania: The collapse of the South Fork Dam left more than 2,200 people dead.

May 25, 1979, Chicago, Illinois: An American Airlines DC-10 plane crashed seconds after takeoff. All 272 people aboard and three people on the ground were killed.

March 24, 1989, Prince William Sound, Alaska: The *Exxon Valdez* hit an underwater reef and released more than 10 million gallons of oil into the water (below). No people died, but thousands of birds, fish, otters, and other animals were killed or hurt.

Below are some of the deadliest natural disasters in U.S. history.

October 8, 1871, Peshtigo, Wisconsin: More than 1,500 lives were lost and 3.8 million acres were burned in a forest fire.

September 8, 1900, Galveston, Texas: A hurricane struck the island on which Galveston is located. Between ten and twelve thousand people died—six to eight thousand in Galveston alone. The exact numbers will never be known. This was the biggest disaster in U.S. history in terms of loss of life.

April 18, 1906, San Francisco, California: An earthquake followed by a fire destroyed more than four square miles of San Francisco, including all the buildings in the area (above right). More than five hundred people died.

March 18, 1925, Missouri, Illinois, and Indiana: The great Tri-State Tornado left 689 people dead and more than 2,000 injured. Property damage was estimated at $16.5 million—a tremendous sum at the time.

Communities like New Orleans rely on the National Flood Insurance Program to recover from disaster.

houses or offices. The government encourages people to install smoke alarms. This warns people right away when a fire is burning. It also requires people to evacuate their homes or workplaces before a hurricane

DHS employees work hard to predict what terrorists will do next. If they do their jobs well, disasters like 9/11 will not happen again.

strikes. FEMA educates citizens and emergency workers around the country in the many different ways disasters can be prevented or minimized.

Prevent Disasters from Occurring

Not all man-made disasters, such as terrorist attacks, can be prevented. Still, DHS employees work hard to predict what terrorists will do next. If they do their jobs well, disasters like 9/11 will not happen again. If a terrorist attack does occur again, people will be better prepared.

Natural disasters can be difficult to prevent, too. Earthquakes often hit without warning. Even weather-related disasters such as hurricanes can only be predicted, not prevented. Some disasters, such as fires, can be prevented. FEMA employees educate people about how to prevent fires at home, in public places, or even in the forest.

FEMA staff in Atlanta, Georgia, prepare for the arrival of Hurricane Dennis in July 2005. They provide up-to-date information to disaster workers on the front lines.

Chapter 3

Careers on the Front Lines of Emergency Management

Who are first responders, and what do they do? First responders are police, firefighters, and emergency medical technicians (EMTs). People everywhere rely on these specialists. What would happen if we could not count on their skills? For one thing, many Americans would not be alive today. First responders help victims of car accidents, fires, and natural disasters—to name just a few of the emergencies that keep them busy.

First responders are on duty twenty-four hours a day, seven days a week. They usually do not work directly for FEMA, but they are closely connected to the agency. FEMA makes sure that the nation's first responders are well educated. FEMA also makes sure they have the right equipment to do their job. Overall, it makes sure first responders are well prepared to act in any emergency. Some first responders work on FEMA's Urban Search and Rescue teams when they are called into action.

It is impossible to feature all the careers in emergency management. Instead, this chapter highlights three of the better-known first-responder professions: urban search and rescue specialist, emergency medical technician, and firefighter. It also takes a look at FEMA's disaster assistance employees. These are special jobs on the front line of disasters.

Urban Search and Rescue Specialist

The 9/11 terrorist attacks put the spotlight on FEMA's US&R task forces (also called US&R teams). After the World Trade Center towers collapsed, the news showed pictures of these workers searching carefully through the rubble. People all over the world witnessed their courage. What is it like to be a member of these teams? What do they do? Here is a true story about another time when US&R teams were called to action.

The Oklahoma City Bombing

Dr. Brian Espe is a veterinarian. In 1995, he was working for the U.S. Department of Agriculture.[1] On the morning of April 19, 1995 he went to his office at the Alfred P. Murrah Building in Oklahoma City. He had just started his workday when he heard a loud rumble. Then he heard nothing but a sickening silence. He realized that the building had collapsed. He was trapped.

It took more than an hour for search and rescue crews to reach Espe and get him out of the building. Espe was afraid of heights. This made it difficult for him to climb down the ladder to safety. Firefighter Mark

Mulman helped him overcome that fear and rescued him from the wreckage. Images of Espe's rescue show the horror of the worst terrorist attack on U.S. soil up to that time. These pictures show Espe moving slowly down a ladder and out of the building. "Thank God for Mark," said Espe of the firefighter who helped him, "because he talked me down every step of the way."[2]

The facts of the Oklahoma City bombing became clearer in the hours after the attack. At 9:02 that

---

The first rescue workers from Oklahoma City's fire department entered the building just after the explosion. Most of the steel support system had been blown out.

---

morning, a bomb exploded inside a rented moving truck parked under the building. The blast nearly caused all nine floors of the building to collapse. The first rescue workers from the city's fire department entered the building just after the explosion. They were not sure if it could continue to support its own weight. Most of the steel support system had been blown out.[3]

The first FEMA US&R teams were at the scene within five hours of the blast.[4] They began their

On April 19, 1995, a bomb blasted the Alfred P. Murrah Federal Building in Oklahoma City. FEMA's Urban Search and Rescue teams rushed to the scene.

gruesome task with the help of search and rescue dogs. These dogs are trained to bark when they find live victims. Over the next few days, eleven of FEMA's twenty-seven US&R teams worked at the site. (Today there are twenty-eight teams.) FEMA teams worked with local fire departments, police departments, the military, and other federal agencies during the search and rescue effort. Together they combed through the rubble. They looked for survivors in tight, dark spaces. They also stabilized the badly damaged building.

One hundred sixty-eight people died in the Oklahoma City bombing. Nineteen of the dead were children. Still, search and rescue teams pulled dozens of survivors from the rubble. Through their heroic efforts, they kept the death toll from rising.

Who Is Part of FEMA's US&R Teams?

As you know, US&R teams are called in when people become trapped in a building or other structure. Every search and rescue assignment is unique. Still, events usually follow a similar pattern.[5] The first response to an emergency begins at the local level. If the situation is very serious, the local emergency manager asks for help from the state. The state may ask for federal assistance. Once the president declares a disaster,

FEMA sends its three closest US&R task forces right away. More teams are sent if the situation requires it.

Engineers act as structural specialists for FEMA. After arriving at the disaster site, these specialists find out how strong the structure is after the disaster. They determine whether the structure is likely to collapse completely.

Members of the search group have a difficult task. Often they must break and cut through thousands of pounds of concrete, metal, and wood to reach the person.

The search team moves around and into the damaged structure. Team members support it to prevent further damage. They stabilize the entry and work areas. The team uses electronic listening devices, search cameras, and specially trained search dogs to locate trapped victims. Once a victim is located, members of the search group have a difficult task. Often they must break and cut through thousands of pounds of concrete, metal, and wood to reach the person.

Medical teams include doctors, nurses, and paramedics. They provide medical care for victims and rescuers. They work in a mobile emergency room.

Medical teams may need to enter the dangerous structure to give first aid.

During the rescue operation, hazardous materials specialists check the disaster site. They look for dangerous chemicals and other hazards. Rigging specialists direct the use of heavy machinery such as cranes and bulldozers. These people understand the

These US&R team members specialize in hazardous materials (yellow hat), survivor rescue (red hat), and medical care (blue hat).

FEMA US&R task forces use an equipment cache, or supply.[6] This cache allows the task force to be self-sufficient for up to three days. The cache is huge—it weighs nearly 60,000 pounds and costs about $1.4 million. Together, the task-force members and their cache would fill a giant military transport plane (right).[7]

Team members called logistics specialists take care of the 16,400 pieces of equipment in the cache. The cache is both a mobile emergency room and a construction site. It is also a communications center and a high-tech engineering firm. The cache is a campsite, too. The task force has everything it needs, so it does not have to ask the struggling community for supplies. The cache includes sleeping bags, cots, food, water, and cold- or wet-weather gear.

What kind of medical supplies are in the cache? It has medicine, fluids, blankets, and materials for stitching wounds. Tubes to restore breathing and defibrillators are available. Burn treatments, bone saws, and scalpels are there as well.

Search and rescue equipment is a lot like tools found at a construction site. There are concrete saws, jackhammers, drills, lumber, and rope. These are used to remove victims safely and slowly from the rubble.

Communications gear allows rescuers to stay in touch with others. This is especially important when they locate a victim. Lights, radios, cell phones, computers, and other electronic equipment are available in the cache.

More than five hundred tools make up the technical support cache. For example, there are cameras and scopes attached to long, thin devices. These can move through rubble like a snake to send images back to the rescuers. Super-sensitive listening devices can detect even the slightest human sound. These high-tech tools may help locate survivors.

dangers of working in a weakened structure. They help ensure the safety of the people inside—both the victims and the rescuers.

Information and communication specialists ensure that all team members can communicate with each other and the team leaders. They help organize an evacuation if the building shows signs of further collapse. Logistics specialists take care of the equipment used to support the rescue operation.

As you can see, a task force includes many people with special skills. How can you prepare for a career on one of FEMA's twenty-eight hardworking US&R task forces?

Becoming a US&R Specialist

To become a US&R specialist, you must already be a disaster or emergency management specialist. For example, a task-force member might be a firefighter or a canine (dog) search and rescue handler. Another team member could be an engineer. This person works with buildings and other structures. Medical doctors and paramedics also join the teams. Most task-force members already have full-time jobs. They are called away from their regular work in times of need. FEMA usually recruits US&R team members from local emergency forces. The agency announces available positions on its Web site.

Training requirements for the task forces are strict. US&R is hazardous work that involves hundreds of

Search and Rescue Specialist

A US&R dog joins FEMA workers as they fly to New Orleans after Hurricane Katrina.

hours of training. People must take courses with written tests. Practice exercises are also part of the training. The need for US&R task forces has never been greater. Task-force members can expect to earn a salary and benefits that vary according to their skills.

Part of the Team: Urban Search and Rescue Dogs
Search and rescue dogs and their handlers are part of every US&R task force.[8] They are a good example of the strict training needed to be part of these special teams.

Canine specialists and their handlers go through strict training before they can join FEMA.

Highly trained search and rescue dogs are called canine specialists. They know how to move safely into collapsed structures to search an area carefully. They are trained to locate trapped people. They know how to alert their handlers when they find something of interest. These special dogs work hard to save human lives.

A canine–handler team must be trained and certified in search and rescue before it can join a US&R task force. A person does not need experience with

---

Highly trained search and rescue dogs are called canine specialists. These special dogs work hard to save human lives.

---

dogs to become a canine handler. It is helpful, however, to like animals and to have some experience working with them.

Both the handler and the dog must meet tough requirements. They must earn basic and advanced certificates. To earn a basic certificate, the search dog must be able to do certain things. For example, it must be able to climb safely through rubble and to locate a victim with the handler's help. An advanced certificate requires the search dog to locate a victim without the handler. The dog must also be able to do a successful

search of more difficult rescue courses. These courses are practice sites designed to teach the dog its job.

Canine–handler teams must be recertified every two years to participate in search and rescue. This means they must always train to keep up their skills. Almost 85 percent of FEMA's US&R canine handlers are volunteers. The remaining 15 percent are members of a local fire or police department. Nearly all the canines are considered family dogs, and they usually live with their handlers. They often work until they become too old. Then they help to train a younger dog to replace them.

After the 9/11 attacks, as many as eighty FEMA search dogs were active at Ground Zero. Another twenty took part in the rescue efforts at the Pentagon. In fact, the US&R effort at Ground Zero was the largest deployment of search dogs in U.S. history. In addition to the FEMA canines, there were dogs from the New York City Police Department K9 Corps. Search dogs from around the country were there as well. In total, nearly four hundred dogs were active in the 9/11 response efforts.

Like the other members of the US&R task forces at Ground Zero, search dogs were on call for twelve-hour shifts. Generally the dogs worked on the rubble pile for twenty to forty-five minutes. Then they would rest for an equal period of time. The conditions were dangerous at Ground Zero, but few search dogs were seriously hurt and none died.

During a search and rescue operation like 9/11, one of a handler's main responsibilities is to maintain the interest and spirit of the dogs. For the dogs, a search is almost like a game of hide-and-seek. Locating a person, called a find, is the reward. Sometimes a dog has a long period without a find. When this happens, the handler may have a team member hide and send the dog out to search. This way the dog has a successful find and keeps up its spirit.

Emergency Medical Technician (EMT)

Anyone who has watched *ER* on television knows the important role EMTs play in providing urgent care to patients. Are you looking for a career that can truly have a positive impact on people's lives? Then this challenging job could be just right for you. It may also lead you toward a position on a FEMA support team or US&R team.[9]

EMTs bring medical care to victims of disasters and accidents. They help stabilize people with medical emergencies until they can be taken to a doctor or hospital. EMTs may need to gain control over a victim's bleeding, apply bandages or splints, or provide oxygen. They may have to resuscitate a victim—that means they help the victim start breathing again.

Sometimes EMTs treat people for shock or assist in an unexpected childbirth. They also may treat poisoning or burns.

Emergency medical technicians (EMTs) are often first to arrive after disasters and accidents.

They might also help rescue people trapped by a fire. Once victims are stable, EMTs transport them to a hospital. These are only a few of the things an EMT may do on the job.

EMTs work for local fire departments, ambulance companies, hospitals, and police departments. Some find work fighting forest fires. Others work at parks and recreation areas, and even at amusement parks.

EMTs must be able to give and receive spoken and written instructions quickly and clearly. They must be able to remain calm in emergencies. They have to maintain a neat, clean, and professional appearance. EMTs must use good judgment under stress and have common sense. They need to know how to drive an emergency vehicle. It is difficult to care for and transport an injured person. EMTs are trained to avoid causing more injury to patients as they try to help them.

Are you thinking of becoming an EMT? It is a good idea to take as many high-school courses as possible in biology, chemistry, and health. Even a driver's-education class is worthwhile. A high-school diploma or general equivalency diploma (GED) is usually the minimum requirement for an EMT career.

You may also want to consider volunteering with an ambulance or a rescue squad. This will give you valuable real-world experience. Many volunteer units offer training in emergency medical skills. As a volunteer, you may learn first aid and cardiopulmonary resuscitation (CPR). You can also learn these skills by

CPR is a skill that saves thousands of lives in the United States. More than 5 million Americans learn how to do CPR every year.[10] Both the American Heart Association and the American Red Cross offer courses in CPR. EMTs know CPR and many more medical techniques. CPR is also useful for people without advanced medical training.

CPR can help a person who has stopped breathing or has had a cardiac arrest. Cardiac arrest means the heart has stopped beating. Sudden cardiac arrest is the leading cause of death in adults. It usually happens in people's homes. People who know CPR can save a person's life until he or she is taken to the hospital.

What kinds of emergencies would make knowing CPR useful? If someone's heart stops beating because of a heart attack, CPR may save his life. If someone has nearly drowned, CPR could help her start breathing again. If the heart stops, the absence of oxygen in the blood can cause brain damage in just minutes. Death will occur within eight to ten minutes. Studies show that CPR helps most when it is started as soon as possible after cardiac arrest. Trained medical personnel should arrive within eight to twelve minutes.

CPR involves two techniques. First is rescue breathing, also known as mouth-to-mouth breathing. It brings air to a person's lungs when he or she has stopped breathing. Rescuers place their mouth tightly over a victim's mouth. Then they forcefully blow air

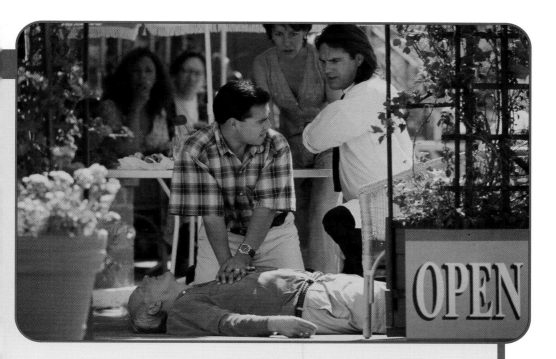

into the victim's lungs. The other technique is called chest compression. (To compress means to press or squeeze.) It helps keep blood flowing to the body's vital organs, such as the brain and lungs. To perform chest compression, a person who knows CPR presses down on a victim's chest. The rescuer positions his or her hands in a specific way over the breastbone. When performed correctly, the compressions cause blood to be pumped from the heart to other organs.

If someone at an emergency scene knows CPR, he or she can double the chances that a victim will survive. If performed incorrectly, it may not work—and it can even be harmful. Would you like to learn CPR? Consider taking a first-aid training course. Who knows? You may save a life—and it could prepare you for a career in emergency management.

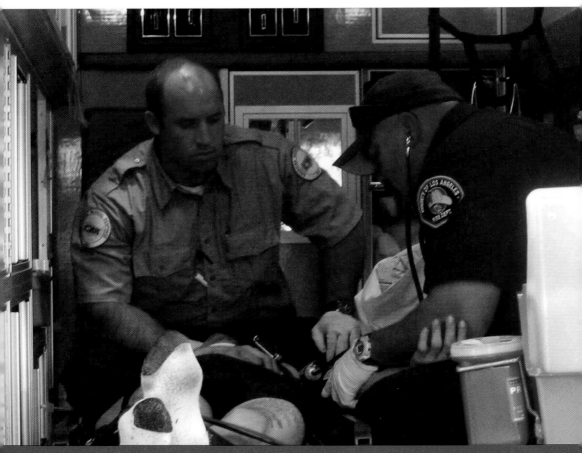

Paramedics treat a victim in Los Angeles County. These EMTs have reached the most advanced level of their profession.

taking courses with the American Heart Association or the Red Cross.

If you want to become an EMT, consider enrolling in a basic EMT training program after completing high school. These programs include 110 to 120 hours of classroom instruction and a ten-hour internship at a

Search and Rescue Specialist

hospital. Police, fire departments, and state health departments offer these programs. All fifty states require that people have this basic training before they can become an EMT. You must then pass the EMT-basic written and practical exams. The states give these tests. So does an organization called the National

---

Salaries for EMTs generally start at minimum wage. Full-time EMTs working for a private ambulance company can expect to earn between $20,000 and $40,000 per year.

Registry of Emergency Medical Technicians. Once you pass the test, you become a registered EMT-basic. The next level of practice, EMT-intermediate, requires an additional thirty-five to fifty-five hours in the classroom and more advanced work in the field.

The most advanced level of EMT is registered EMT-paramedic. This level requires a strict program of coursework and internships. Then the person takes a state test or the National Registry EMT-Paramedic Exam.

Salaries for EMTs generally start at minimum wage. Full-time EMTs working for a private ambulance company can expect to earn between $20,000 and $40,000 per year. EMTs who work for a city's fire department tend to make more money. They usually have better benefits and working conditions, too.

There will be a growing need for EMTs in the future. Today we know more about how important emergency medical care can be. Any help a victim receives before arriving at the hospital may save a life. Most fire departments now require their firefighters to have EMT training, too.

They do not work directly for FEMA, but EMTs are an important part of U.S. disaster response forces. EMTs often move on to become firefighters or to join FEMA's US&R teams.

Firefighter

Firefighters protect communities against injury, loss of life, and destruction of property from fires. This is a large part of their job. Today's firefighters are also called on to rescue people in situations other than fires. These include car accidents and medical emergencies, such as a heart attack or near drowning. Firefighters may also rescue people after a terrorist attack.[11]

Are you interested in becoming a firefighter? Many people would like to work in this exciting career. It is competitive, so it can be tough to get the job. Make sure to earn at least a high-school diploma or GED. Fire departments across the United States are looking for people who have brains as well as brawn. Some fire departments require firefighters to have a college degree. Today colleges offer courses in the investigation

The job of a firefighter is risky but exciting. Here, firefighters put out flames at Ground Zero after the 9/11 attacks.

of arson (fires that people start on purpose) and in fire science. These courses may help you become a firefighter. A college education may also open the door for future opportunities—such as working for FEMA.

Many people call fire departments for medical emergencies. Fire departments often hire employees who are trained as both firefighters and EMTs. Basic CPR classes and other emergency medical training are a smart choice. Firefighters must pass a difficult test of strength and stamina. Once hired, firefighters have to stay in top physical shape. They must also have a medical exam that includes testing for drug use.

What do real firefighters do on the job? Find out before choosing this career. It is difficult work. Sign up as a volunteer for a local fire department. This is a great way to learn about the job. Meet with the chief of the department. Talk to him or her about the requirements for volunteers. More information is also available on the National Volunteer Fire Council's Web site.

Once hired, firefighters complete their training program. They also take firefighting exams. Many departments have a two- to four-month program of classes and training. These classes cover firefighting skills and fire prevention. New recruits also learn how to handle dangerous materials. They learn emergency medical skills as well.

Training may be followed by a trial period of employment. This can last from three to six months.

Search and Rescue Specialist

During this time, the department decides whether the recruit will be a good team member. If not, the recruit may be let go. Firefighters must be able to work together as a team.

Firefighters are responsible for taking good care of their equipment.

To ensure that all their equipment works properly, firefighters are responsible for taking care of their trucks, the fire station, and their emergency equipment. They work both indoors and outdoors. Some fight wildfires during the spring and summer seasons. All perform work

> Firefighters work long hours in dangerous conditions. They may be required to eat, sleep, and work at a fire station while on duty.

in physically and mentally challenging situations. They work long hours in dangerous conditions. If they are part of a local fire department, they may be required to eat, sleep, and work at a fire station while on duty. For example, they may work (and sleep) at the station for forty-eight hours at a time. Then they will have three days off.

What firefighters earn depends on the type and size of their department. Larger cities usually pay more than midsize and smaller cities. City departments also offer more chances for assignments such as fire inspector or fire investigator. A fire inspector checks for fire hazards in a business or home. A fire investigator looks into cases of arson to find out who may be involved in the crime.

In a large city, the salary of a new firefighter can range from $2,000 to $6,000 per month. Firefighters with several years of experience may earn between $4,000 and $8,000 per month. Firefighters usually receive excellent benefits, including a paid retirement plan and health insurance.

Search and Rescue Specialist

Experienced firefighters will always find plenty of opportunities to move ahead in their careers. Some may become a member of a FEMA US&R team. Others will be promoted to chief of a fire department. Still others may find they enjoy training other emergency workers. Firefighting is one of the most dangerous careers, but it is also one of the most rewarding ones.

A firefighter tries to put out a forest fire in Montana in 2003.

FEMA's Disaster Assistance Employees

Disaster assistance employees, or DAEs, work for FEMA as temporary employees.[12] They help out on the front lines of FEMA operations. FEMA employs about four thousand DAEs. The number varies depending on how many emergencies there are at a given time. Working as a DAE is not a full-time job. Still, it is a good way for someone interested in emergency management to see what the work is like. Some DAEs get full-time jobs within FEMA after they have worked for a while in the field.

DAEs are called to action when the president officially declares a disaster. There are two categories of DAEs. The first category is local people from the place where disaster strikes. The second is FEMA reservists. These employees do not live in the area. Instead they are called to work when a disaster strikes. Then they travel to the area.

DAEs usually report to the disaster field office. This command post is set up in the disaster area. The disaster field office sends DAEs to do whatever is needed. They may help people find housing or organize food and medication. They may help people fill out paperwork to receive financial aid. Their main goal is to make people's lives as normal as possible.

DAEs work directly on the front lines. They work side by side with relief workers from local and state governments and other organizations. DAEs know they have lent a helping hand to people in need—victims of

FEMA/STATE
DISASTER RECOVERY
CENTER

Disaster assistance employee (DAE) positions are open to almost anyone. These DAEs help victims of Hurricane Dennis in Alabama.

disasters and emergencies. This is a very satisfying feeling. There are other benefits to these positions, too. DAEs are paid by the hour. They receive overtime pay when they work more than eight hours a day or forty hours a week. Those who travel to the disaster site are paid for travel and living expenses.

How much DAEs earn depends on their skills and experience. There are different levels of DAEs. People with less experience are paid about $10 per hour. Those with the most skills and experience earn about $40 per hour. Many DAEs work fifty- to sixty-hour weeks.

The qualifications to be a DAE are minimal. People do not need a high-school diploma or a college degree. The jobs are open to most people who want to help. You can apply by following the instructions on FEMA's Web site. You can also apply at a local FEMA disaster field office in an area where a disaster has struck.

All FEMA employees must perform their jobs to the best of their abilities—especially when disaster strikes. This worker is preparing generators needed after Hurricane Dennis in 2005.

Chapter 4

Careers Inside FEMA

Now it is time to look behind the scenes of emergency management. In this chapter you will learn more about what people do inside FEMA. Working at the scene of a disaster is not for everyone, but hundreds of jobs behind the scenes are available, too. These workers are just as important as the people on the front lines.

As you learned earlier, FEMA has about 2,600 permanent, full-time staff. This may seem like a lot, but it is a pretty small workforce compared with most government agencies. Still, numerous jobs are available. This book cannot provide a full list of all the careers in FEMA. Instead it highlights a few of them. It provides information on how to find out more about working for FEMA.

Individual Assistance Program Management Chief

What is an Individual Assistance Program management chief? People in this position manage DAEs and other FEMA resources. They take charge of the agency's

A few ground rules apply to all careers in FEMA. In fact, these rules apply to nearly any public-service job with the government.

First, the federal government is an equal opportunity employer. This means that when people apply for a job with FEMA, they will not be discriminated against because of race, national origin, sex, age, political beliefs, or physical handicaps. (Some jobs, such as US&R team member, require total mobility, however.) There is one exception: Most FEMA employees must be U.S. citizens or nationals (a national is a person under the country's protection but not an official citizen). In rare cases, FEMA and other agencies are allowed to hire noncitizens. This happens only when no citizen qualified for the job is available.

Do you think you might want to work for the government one day? Then you should keep out of trouble now. A criminal record definitely counts against people who apply for a government job. Candidates for most of these jobs may have to take a urine test to establish whether or not they have been using any drugs. The government does not hire people who use illegal drugs.

Many FEMA employees may be called to work at any hour, day or night, in the event of an emergency. They may have to travel to the scene of a disaster and stay there for weeks or months. FEMA workers must be able to go to emergency sites with little notice. They also have to be able to work under physical and mental stress.

Individual Assistance Program (IAP). This program helps people recover from a disaster as quickly as possible. IAP chiefs oversee the people who help victims. They work with other FEMA staff and also with other agencies. Together they decide what should be done to help people. The IAP chief works to send what is needed to get the job done.

You have learned that FEMA helps people immediately after disaster strikes. Services also may be offered long after the disaster. Imagine that a family's

---

```
Imagine that a family's house
is destroyed by a hurricane.
With help from the IAP the
family finds temporary
housing. Later the program
helps the family find more
permanent housing.
```

---

house is destroyed by a hurricane. With help from the IAP the family finds temporary housing. Later, the program helps the family find more permanent housing. Sometimes this is not possible until many months later because the disaster has caused so much damage. An IAP chief's teams will stay on the case until the community gets back to normal—however long that takes.

IAP chiefs must be organized and have excellent communication skills. They may work long hours on the job. They may need to travel to a disaster area. A college education is required for the position. A degree in emergency management would be a good idea. Studying public health is another option. Public health is the science of protecting the public's health with preventive medicine, education, disease control, and other skills. Firsthand experience in disaster response may also help someone get this job. Experienced firefighters and EMTs are good candidates for IAP management chief positions. The salary ranges between $50,000 and $85,000 per year.

Mapping Technical Specialist

FEMA's Mapping and Analysis Center is located in Washington, D.C. An operations manager runs this center. He or she supervises a small team of mapping technical specialists. Their job is to make maps and to provide Geographic Information System (GIS) services to FEMA and other agencies.

GIS is a computer database system. It uses software to create and display maps and tables. GIS data is used to help make decisions during emergencies. It can show rescuers where victims are located. It can tell them where local hospitals, schools, and fire stations are. GIS systems map out roads in the area and show what the weather is doing. These are just a few examples of the information GIS can provide.

Mapping specialists gather data from various sources. Two of these are the Bureau of the Census and

A mapping technical specialist prints out his work at the Mapping and Analysis Center in Washington, D.C.

the U.S. Geological Survey. The specialists then use the data to create computerized and paper maps.

During the hurricanes of 2004, the Mapping and Analysis Center produced more than two thousand maps. The maps were used to help rescue people who were trapped. They helped people ship and distribute food, water, and other supplies to the right place. They were used to keep watch over the hurricanes, high winds, flooding, and damage. They were also used to

Mapping specialists must be skilled at working with computers and statistics.

track the location of FEMA workers and to keep them safe. FEMA managers use GIS maps to make quick decisions. The maps allow them to find the best way to help people in an emergency.

What does it take to become a mapping technical specialist? These FEMA employees know a lot about computers and statistical analysis. Statistical analysis uses math and other methods to understand large amounts of information. For example, by looking at statistics, they can compare an event like a hurricane

2004 Multiple Storms

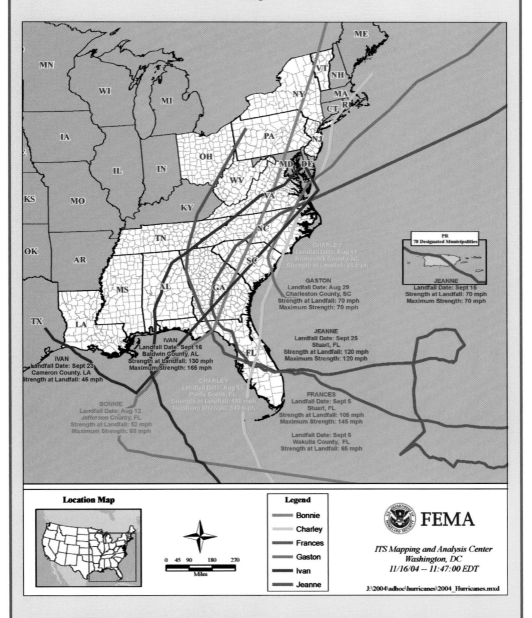

CHARLEY
Landfall Date: Aug 13
Brunswick County, NC
Strength at Landfall: 75 mph

GASTON
Landfall Date: Aug 29
Charleston County, SC
Strength at Landfall: 70 mph
Maximum Strength: 70 mph

JEANNE
Landfall Date: Sept 25
Stuart, FL
Strength at Landfall: 120 mph
Maximum Strength: 120 mph

IVAN
Landfall Date: Sept 16
Baldwin County, AL
Strength at Landfall: 130 mph
Maximum Strength: 165 mph

IVAN
Landfall Date: Sept 23
Cameron County, LA
Strength at Landfall: 45 mph

BONNIE
Landfall Date: Aug 12
Jefferson County, FL
Strength at Landfall: 52 mph
Maximum Strength: 68 mph

CHARLEY
Landfall Date: Aug 13
Punta Gorda, FL
Strength at Landfall: 140 mph
Maximum Strength: 140 mph

FRANCES
Landfall Date: Sept 5
Stuart, FL
Strength at Landfall: 105 mph
Maximum Strength: 145 mph

Landfall Date: Sept 6
Wakulla County, FL
Strength at Landfall: 65 mph

PR
78 Designated Municipalities

JEANNE
Landfall Date: Sept 15
Strength at Landfall: 70 mph
Maximum Strength: 70 mph

Location Map

0   45 90   180   270
Miles

Legend
- Bonnie
- Charley
- Frances
- Gaston
- Ivan
- Jeanne

FEMA

ITS Mapping and Analysis Center
Washington, DC
11/16/04 -- 11:47:00 EDT

J:\2004\adhoc\hurricanes\2004_Hurricanes.mxd

FEMA created a map to predict the path of hurricanes in 2004. This helped the agency mitigate the effects of these natural disasters.

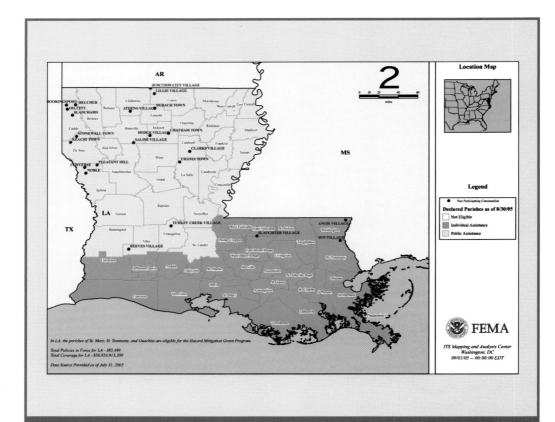

Geographic Information System (GIS) maps come from powerful computers. This map shows communities affected by Hurricane Katrina.

with what has happened over the past hundred years and see how unusual the event is. Knowledge of geography is necessary for this job, too. A college degree in a related area is required. Some experience in mapping and work on GIS projects is recommended.

FEMA's Mapping and Analysis Center is not large. Few mapping jobs are available, but there is a growing demand for these specialists. Mapping specialists earn between $45,000 and $85,000 per year. The salary depends on their background and experience.

About the Geographic Information System

FEMA used GIS for many years before Hurricane Andrew struck in 1992.[1] Then the hurricane made it clear just how useful a tool it can be. GIS helped FEMA and the state of Florida work more effectively to help people during and after the disaster. After that, FEMA began to use GIS more than ever.

During the 1993 Midwest floods, FEMA used GIS to map real-time flood information. This allowed people to see how much damage the floods had caused moment by moment. In 1994, FEMA used GIS during the California earthquakes. That same year, FEMA opened its Mapping and Analysis Center. This high-tech GIS laboratory supports FEMA's workers at the scene of a disaster, as well as other employees at the agency.

Soon after a disaster, FEMA managers and staff can use GIS to see the damage. They can look at images taken from the air and the ground. They can find out who has been affected by the disaster. They can determine which resources (such as water and electricity) are in trouble. FEMA then uses this information to send food and supplies and to work with other organizations.

Emergency Management Specialist

Many full-time positions at FEMA are called emergency management specialist (EMS). Each position has a different set of responsibilities. Some specialists prepare communities to handle a disaster. Others focus on disaster response or recovery. Each regional office usually has several EMSs. They can also be found at FEMA's headquarters.

```
It takes a lot of work
   to run an emergency
training exercise. The
EMS has to be up-to-date
on the latest skills and
   equipment in the
     rescue field.
```

Here is an example of something an EMS might do. We will take a look at the work of an EMS assigned to the Assessment and Exercise Team. This team develops training exercise programs. The programs teach federal, state, and local emergency-management teams how to respond to emergencies.

It takes a lot of work to run an emergency training exercise. The EMS has to be up-to-date on the latest skills and equipment in the rescue field. This way participants get the best information. The EMS obtains the supplies needed to run the training exercises. Then he or she organizes the supplies and the participants before the program begins. After the exercise, the EMS decides if it was a success. Are corrections and improvements necessary? Training exercises are very important. They keep emergency workers prepared.

Emergency management specialists (EMSs) take care of the many day-to-day details involved in disaster response work.

EMSs need many skills. They must have knowledge and experience in their field. They must be able to understand laws and regulations. They need to communicate well, whether they are speaking to a coworker or teaching a course to a large group. They need to be able to write clearly, whether it is a short letter or a long report for an important official. A college degree is not necessary to qualify for the job, but it helps to be successful in this field.

There is a growing need for trained and skilled EMSs. They can earn between $45,000 and $85,000 a year. Their salary depends on their skills, background, and experience.

Director of Regional Operations

There are several senior management positions at FEMA. One of them is the director of regional operations. This person works in Washington, D.C. He or she works closely with FEMA's ten regional offices. The director offers them guidance and leadership. He or she also keeps other FEMA officials aware of any issues or concerns that people at the regional offices may have. The regional offices are responsible for implementing FEMA's programs and policies in the fifty states and the U.S. territories. They also respond to disasters that strike the communities in their areas.

To become a director of regional operations—or any other top managerial position at FEMA—a college

FEMA's training specialists work at the Emergency Management Institute in Emmitsburg, Maryland.

degree is highly recommended. A degree in business or emergency management is useful. A manager at FEMA earns between $75,000 and $115,000 a year.

Training Specialist

A FEMA training specialist trains people to work in disaster management. These specialists work at FEMA's Emergency Management Institute in Emmitsburg, Maryland. You have learned that FEMA trains first responders such as firefighters and police officers. It also provides training for its own staff and volunteers. Some

A training specialist teaches students how to respond to fires quickly.

courses are delivered on the Internet. Others are held in classrooms at the Emergency Management Institute.

Training specialists must be skilled in many aspects of disaster management. Otherwise it would be difficult for them to teach effective classes. They usually work for FEMA in other positions before they accept this job. Salaries for training specialists range from $50,000 to $100,000 a year.

Public Affairs Specialist

Most of FEMA's regional offices employ public affairs specialists. These employees also work at the Washington headquarters. Like many FEMA employees, public affairs team members help people after a disaster. They make sure victims receive all the information they need to return their lives to normal. Many people who are affected by a disaster do not know where to turn for help. Public affairs specialists talk to the media to give out this information.

A college degree in a field such as journalism may help interested candidates join FEMA's public affairs team. Salaries range between $50,000 and $80,000 per year depending on experience.

Program Support Assistant

FEMA's program support assistants do not need a college degree. They do need to be organized and have certain clerical skills, however. For example, they must know how to use word-processing and other computer programs. They need to know how to type, file papers, maintain calendars for executives, and answer telephone inquiries. Communication skills are vital for this job. Program support positions are available at all FEMA offices. Salaries range between $30,000 and $45,000 per year, depending on experience and skills.

Flood Insurance Program Specialist

Flood Insurance Program specialists work in FEMA's regional offices. They run the Flood Mitigation Assistance Program. They also provide assistance to states and communities that take part in the National Flood Insurance Program. Insurance can protect homeowners and businesses in places where floods are likely to happen. If property is damaged, insurance provides money to repair or replace it.

Insurance program specialists know what parts of the country are at high risk of flooding. They make sure people who live there have the insurance they need. To qualify for this job, a college degree is recommended. Most Flood Insurance Program specialists work in the insurance business before they apply for a job with FEMA. Salaries range between $45,000 and $90,000.

Civil Engineer

Civil engineers plan and direct the construction of bridges, roads, harbors, canals, dams, and other public works. FEMA engineers work in the agency's regional

FEMA Jobs and Salaries

Job Title	Requires College Degree?	Salary Range
Disaster assistance employee	No	$10–$40 per hour
Program support assistant	No	$30,000–$45,000
Emergency management specialist	No	$45,000–$85,000
Mapping technical specialist	Yes	$45,000–$85,000
Flood Insurance Program specialist	No	$45,000–$90,000
Public affairs specialist	No	$50,000–$80,000
Individual Assistance Program management chief	Yes	$50,000–$85,000
Training specialist	No	$50,000–$100,000
Civil engineer	Yes	$65,000–$85,000
Director of regional operations	No	$75,000–$115,000

offices. They collect the necessary information to create flood maps. As part of the National Flood Insurance Program, FEMA creates these maps to identify areas at the greatest risk for flooding. Today FEMA can gather better mapmaking information than ever before. The agency has begun making its maps available on the Internet. Civil engineers also work in the field to collect data or to oversee construction projects. Salaries range between $65,000 and $85,000.

Many people start their careers elsewhere to gain necessary experience before working at FEMA. As this picture shows, a FEMA employee must be ready to do many things at once.

Chapter 5

Preparing for Your Career

This chapter provides more information about resources you can use to prepare for a career in emergency management, including a career at FEMA. As you know by now, FEMA works with many other groups—state and local governments, fire departments, law enforcement, volunteer organizations, and private companies. Many of FEMA's current employees once worked for other organizations that respond to disasters. They were already familiar with FEMA, and FEMA was familiar with them. When a position opened up at FEMA, this familiarity helped them get the job. Getting involved with one of these organizations is a great way to start if you have your sights set on a career at FEMA.

Volunteer Opportunities

Volunteering is an excellent way to start out in emergency management. Volunteer work makes people feel good. It is something they can truly be proud of. It also allows people to gain experience. Think about volunteering. The experience you gain may help you

A FEMA Broadcasting Career

Are you interested in a career in television broadcasting? The U.S. Fire Administration (USFA) runs a television station called PREPnet. This name is short for The Preparedness Network. PREPnet is a leader in the technology of distance learning. People in communities nationwide can tune in to training programs in emergency management, fire safety, and responding to terrorist attacks. All programs are open to the public. Viewers can even download PREPnet's programming onto their cell phones, PDAs, and MP3 players.[1]

PREPnet is located at the National Emergency Training Center in Emmitsburg, Maryland. Several DHS agencies work together to create PREPnet's programs. The station has won more than 120 national awards for its programming.[2]

The employee in this photograph is filming a show called National Alert.

decide whether you would enjoy a career in emergency management. If you do not plan on going to college, volunteering is also an excellent way to start a career. You can use your volunteer training and experience when you apply for full-time work at an emergency-management organization or at FEMA.

Here are some of the volunteer opportunities and resources currently available. This is not a complete list. Do your own research to find out more about programs in your area.

> Many fire departments, especially in smaller towns and rural areas, depend on volunteers. They are thankful for any help they receive.

Volunteer Firefighter

Contact your local fire department to find out about its volunteer programs. People at the department can explain how to volunteer. They will tell you when and where training sessions will be. Many fire departments, especially in smaller towns and rural areas, depend on volunteers. They are thankful for any help they receive. Even in big cities, volunteers are always welcome. This is a great way to learn about firefighting.

FEMA depends on help from American citizens to do its job. The agency encourages citizens of all ages and skills to get involved.

After the 9/11 attacks, many Americans wanted to do something. They asked what they could do to make their communities safer. More than ever, Americans wanted to volunteer their time and work with their neighbors to build a stronger nation. For this reason, President Bush created the Citizen Corps. It gives people the chance to participate as volunteers in homeland security efforts in their communities.[3]

FEMA manages the Citizen Corps, but it is organized and run by community-based Citizen Corps Councils. They help to develop community action plans that educate people about what they should do in an emergency. Members of the Citizen Corps Councils consider what possible threats there may be. They identify local resources and organize Citizen Corps programs. The councils include officials from law enforcement, fire, and emergency medical services. Businesses, schools, churches, hospitals, and other groups take part as well.

Search and Rescue Specialist

Citizen Corps volunteers can participate in many programs. They include the following[4]:

- **Volunteers in Police Service Program:** Civilians help local police departments with nonofficial functions. This allows police officers more time for frontline duties in an emergency.

- **Medical Reserve Corps:** Retired doctors and nurses lend a hand during an emergency.

- **Operation TIPS (Terrorist Information and Prevention System):** This system allows millions of American workers to report suspicious activities that may be linked to terrorism or crime. These people may work at airports or docks, for the postal service, or at the local utility company.

- **Neighborhood Watch Programs:** Citizens keep an eye on their neighborhoods to stop crime (right). President Bush added terrorism prevention to the mission of this program.

Fire departments can always use willing volunteers. This firefighter is hard at work near Charlotte, North Carolina.

Search and Rescue Specialist

Junior Firefighter

Some fire departments have special programs for young people in high school. Junior firefighters are trained in the basics of fire fighting and first aid. Once they have successfully completed the training program, they are assigned to a team. Then they are on call twenty-four hours a day, seven days a week, to respond to fires with their team. Junior firefighters back up adult firefighters at the scene of a fire by doing such jobs as running out the hoses and connecting them to fire hydrants. This way the firefighters can

Teenagers volunteer for their fire department in Aniak, Alaska. To participate, they must maintain good grades and promise not to use drugs or alcohol.

concentrate on handling the fire itself. Contact your local fire department to find out if they have a junior firefighter program. See if you qualify to join.

National Volunteer Fire Council (NVFC)

The NVFC represents the interests of the volunteer fire, emergency medical, and rescue services.[5] What kinds of things do members of the council do? They obtain funding for local volunteer fire departments. They also help to educate and train volunteer firefighters. The NVFC has a Web site where you can find information about volunteer firefighting and how to get involved.

Community Emergency Response Team (CERT)

FEMA oversees Community Emergency Response Teams. These special teams are made up entirely of volunteers. They are trained to help first responders.

In a major emergency, first responders are very busy. They cannot give help to everyone who needs it. This is where CERT comes in. Members of these teams are young and old—from teenagers to retired people. They learn basic first aid. They learn how to help with evacuations and other duties that are important in an emergency.

CERT volunteers also help their communities to prepare for an emergency. They teach people what supplies they would need in a disaster. They tell people how to create a family disaster plan. This is a plan to make sure everyone in a family knows what to do if they

Search and Rescue Specialist

Interested community members sign up to join a CERT. It takes two to three months of classes to become part of a team.

become separated. CERT members may also offer training and presentations at high schools.

Anyone can become a CERT member, including teenagers. It only takes a little of your free time. If you become a CERT member, you will do your part to create a safer community for your family and friends.

Would you like to give some of your time to CERT? All you need to do is sign up with the nearest team and attend a CERT training course. This usually includes eight or ten classes held one evening a week for two to

Members of a Community Emergency Response Team (CERT) participate in a training exercise in Florida. They are learning how to respond to disasters in their area.

three months. Once volunteers graduate, they become part of a CERT team. Usually they are assigned to a team that covers their own neighborhood or one nearby. Not all communities have a CERT program. Call your local fire department to find out if there is one in your town. Ask where to sign up for the next class.

What Is a Family Disaster Plan?

Every family should talk about what to do in a disaster. Here are a few things FEMA suggests you discuss with your family[6]:

- **What types of disasters might happen in your area?**
- **What can you do to prepare for these disasters?**
- **What will you do if you are told to evacuate (to leave your home) because of a disaster?**

Consider choosing a place to meet away from your home, in case of a fire. You could meet at a neighbor's house or at the corner of your street. What if your whole neighborhood has to evacuate? Choose a place to meet outside the area. You might pick a good friend or relative's house.

Decide on a place to call to check in if you become separated from your family during a disaster. Make sure everyone in the family knows the phone number of a friend or family member who lives in another state. You should memorize this number. Then you can call that person to say where you are. This way your family can find you.

You could even organize a meeting with the people in your neighborhood to create disaster plans. Find out if someone has a special skill that would be important during an emergency. Does anyone know CPR or first aid? Is there a nurse or doctor in the neighborhood?

American Red Cross

The American Red Cross is probably the best-known disaster-relief organization in the United States. The paid staff of the Red Cross is actually relatively small. In fact, ninety-seven percent of Red Cross workers are volunteers.[7] They serve the needs of local communities in many ways. Some volunteers help people in an emergency. Others donate blood or teach first-aid and CPR courses. Still others deliver emergency messages to members of the military.

Becoming a Red Cross volunteer is easy. Go to the Red Cross Web site to find the chapter near you. Contact the chapter and find out how you can help.

In August 2004, the American Red Cross delivered about nine thousand meals a day to hurricane victims in Punta Gorda, Florida.

American Red Cross volunteers take a break from helping out at the World Trade Center in September 2001.

Advanced Education

FEMA believes classes in emergency management should be taught at colleges and universities across the United States. College students, as well as people working in emergency management, need courses that teach them about emergencies. They can use this information to prepare others. In the end, the more people who are educated about emergencies and disasters, the safer our communities will be.

What can kids do to help in an emergency? First of all, help make sure your family is prepared. Then talk to your teacher about school preparedness. You might also find out whether there is a CERT team in your community. You can learn basic first aid or help with providing information to a community. The bottom line is this: Get involved!

You can even become a FEMA Disaster Action Kid.[8] Disaster Action Kids receive a certificate, become part of a special e-mail group, and receive exciting news and information directly from FEMA on a regular basis. Disaster Action Kids are prepared. They know what items are needed in a disaster supply kit. They know how to protect their pets during a disaster. They also know what to do during each type of disaster. All you need to do to join is read about disasters on the FEMA Web site for kids, do the activities, and test your knowledge.

To give you a headstart, here is a list of some of the items that should be in every family's disaster supply kit:

- canned meat, fruit, and vegetables
- vitamins
- water
- thermometer
- tweezers
- soap
- bandages
- rainproof clothing and shoes
- paper and pencils
- fire extinguisher
- flashlight and extra batteries
- pliers
- garbage bags

More colleges and universities offer emergency-management training than ever before. The Web site of the Emergency Management Institute has a complete list of the colleges and universities that offer courses or degrees in the field.

Continuing Education in Emergency Management

You may start an emergency-management career at college or by working your way up from a volunteer position. Either way, you will need to continue educating yourself about the field on a regular basis.

FEMA trains emergency-management personnel from all over the United States. The National Emergency Training Center in Maryland is the home of several training schools. From volunteers to top professionals, these schools provide educational opportunities for everyone involved in emergency management.

Emergency Management Institute

When disasters and emergencies occur, organizations must work together to protect people and property and to save lives. FEMA's Emergency Management Institute teaches them to work together more effectively. It is part of the United States Fire Administration and is located on the National Emergency Training Center campus.

The institute offers training to government employees. It is also open to people at volunteer organizations and private companies. The institute's goal is to lessen the effects of disasters with education in basic emergency management. The Emergency Management Institute offers training on subjects such as natural hazards (earthquakes, hurricanes,

The Emergency Management Institute's goal is to lessen the effects of disasters with education in basic emergency management.

floods, dam safety), technological hazards (hazardous materials, terrorism), and providing information to the public.

Approximately 5,500 participants attend courses in Maryland each year, and 100,000 people take courses in other parts of the country. Another 150,000 individuals participate in Emergency Management Institute–supported training exercises each year.[9]

National Fire Academy
The National Fire Academy is part of the U.S. Fire Administration, which is a part of FEMA. The U.S. Fire Administration's mission is to reduce loss of life and property due to fire. The National Fire Academy is also part of the National Emergency Training Center. It is located on the campus in Maryland.

A trainee operates distance learning equipment at the National Emergency Training Center in Maryland.

The National Fire Academy works to improve the ability of fire and emergency services to deal with fires. Since 1975, more than 1.4 million students have received training from the academy. With the knowledge they learn from these training programs, students have saved both lives and property.[10]

Firefighters participate in a training simulation at the National Fire Academy. They are responding to a mock structure fire in a fake city.

Search and Rescue Specialist

FEMA's Noble Training Center is the only hospital in the United States dedicated to preparing health care workers for disasters.

Noble Training Center

Although it is located in Alabama, the Noble Training Center is part of the National Emergency Training Center. It is the only hospital in the United States that is used to train health care workers to prepare for and respond to a disaster. The center trains its students in a realistic hospital setting. This helps them practice how they would handle both natural and man-made disasters. The realistic setting lets students train without disrupting activities at a real hospital. The center has classrooms, a computer lab, and two decontamination lanes. These facilities are used to decontaminate people who have been infected with disease or radiation.[11]

Emergency Management Job Opportunities

How many jobs are available in the field of emergency management? There is no quick answer to this question, but here are some facts:

- As you know, FEMA has a workforce of about 2,600 full-time employees. Its standby disaster reserve force includes nearly four thousand people. In addition to FEMA's employees, about three thousand people work in state or local offices that focus on emergency management.
- At the state and local level, many people play a role in emergency management. One example is the operators who answer calls to 911.
- Other agencies besides FEMA employ hundreds of workers who deal with emergency management.
- More than 1 million firefighters work in the United States. This includes volunteers and paid employees.

Private businesses actually employ more emergency managers than anyone else. There is no record of how many people hold this type of job, but it is estimated

Search and Rescue Specialist

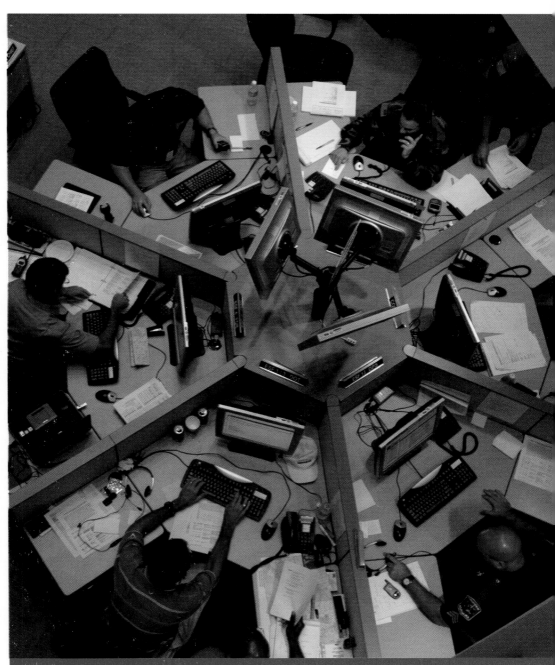
FEMA employs about 2,600 full-time workers. They are stationed at headquarters and at field offices throughout the country.

The nation was shocked by images of Hurricane Katrina in 2005. People throughout the United States realized that disaster preparedness had to be a higher priority.

to be more than a million. Then there are thousands of people who work as volunteers for organizations such as the American Red Cross, but we do not know exactly how many. What we do know is that there will probably be many more emergency management jobs available in the future. The nation's population is growing. The threat of a terrorist attack remains real. Natural disasters, such as Hurricane Katrina in 2005, will continue to take their toll. There will always be a demand for skilled emergency workers.

Natural disasters, such as Hurricane Katrina in 2005, will continue to take their toll. There will always be a demand for skilled emergency workers.

Has this book sparked your interest in emergency management? Has it answered your questions about working for FEMA? Maybe you are thinking of becoming a firefighter or a US&R specialist. Perhaps you would prefer a career as an emergency manager, a mapping specialist, or a civil engineer. There are so many possibilities at FEMA and other organizations. Work hard! The resources you have found here will help you get started on the road to success. Good luck!

Pets in a Disaster

What happens to family pets during a disaster? The Humane Society offers these tips on how to help your pet survive a disaster[12]:

• **If you have to evacuate your home, try not to leave your pets behind.** Pets may not be able to survive on their own. They need someone to feed them and look after them. Even if they do survive, you may not be able to find them when you return.

• **Many emergency shelters cannot take pets.** Find out which motels and hotels in your area allow pets. Your local animal shelter might also be able to provide information about what to do with pets during a disaster.

• **Make sure you have a secure pet carrier or leash for your pets.** In this way, if they panic, they cannot escape.

- **Make sure your pets' ID tags are up-to-date and securely fastened to their collar.** If possible, attach the phone number of the place where you will be staying.

- **Do not forget your pet's supplies—food, bottled water, medications, cat litter and pan, and food dishes.** Consider packing a pet-survival kit that can be used if disaster hits. What would you put in the kit?

- **If you cannot return to your home right away, you may need to board your pet in a kennel or animal shelter.** Most kennels, veterinarians, and animal shelters will need your pet's medical records to make sure the animal is healthy. Include copies in your pet-survival kit along with a photo of your pet.

- **If you cannot take your pet to a temporary shelter, contact friends, family, veterinarians, or kennels to arrange for care.**

Chapter 1. September 11, 2001

1. "September 11: Chronology of Terror," *CNN*, n.d., <http://archives.cnn.com/2001/US/09/11/chronology.attack/> (January 23, 2006). "Timeline: World Trade Center Chronology," *PBS American Experience*, August 22, 2003, <http://www.pbs.org/wgbh/amex/newyork/timeline/timeline2.html> (January 23, 2006).

2. "9/11 by the Numbers," *New York Magazine*, n.d., September 16, 2002, p. 54.

3. George W. Bush, "President Bush's Remarks," *The Washington Post*, September 12, 2001, p. A02.

4. "About US&R," *FEMA.gov*, n.d., <http://www.fema.gov/about/mediausr.shtm> (January 23, 2006).

5. "What You Didn't Know about Urban Search and Rescue," *FEMA.gov*, n.d., <http://www.fema.gov/usr/about1.shtm> (January 25, 2006).

6. "Search and Rescue Teams Active at the World Trade Center and the Pentagon," *FEMA.gov*, n.d., <http://www.fema.gov/remember911/> (January 23, 2006).

7. "Rebuilding Timeline," *Lower Manhattan.info*, n.d., <http://www.lowermanhattan.info/rebuild/timeline/rebuild_timeline_html_2002.asp> (January 23, 2006).

8. "World Trade Center—New York City," *GlobalSecurity.org*, n.d., <http://www.globalsecurity.org/eye/wtc.htm> (May 8, 2006).

Chapter 2. Inside FEMA

1. "FEMA History," *FEMA.gov*, March 21, 2006, <http://www.fema.gov/about/history.shtm> (May 8, 2006). "Statement by Secretary of Homeland Security Michael Chertoff Before the House Government Reform Committee," *Department of*

Homeland Security, June 9, 2005, <http://www.dhs.gov/dhspublic/display?theme=45&content=4536> (May 5, 2006).

2. "FAQs," *Department of Homeland Security*, n.d., <http://www.dhs.gov/dhspublic/faq.jsp> (January 23, 2006).

3. "DHS Organization," *Department of Homeland Security*, January 24, 2006, <http://www.dhs.gov/dhspublic/interapp/editorial/editorial_0515.xml> (May 8, 2006).

4. "FEMA History."

5. "1980 Federal Disaster Declarations," *FEMA.gov*, December 5, 2005, <http://www.fema.gov/news/disasters.fema?year=1980> (May 8, 2006).

6. "Learn About the Types of Disasters," *FEMA.gov*, April 26, 2006, <http://www.fema.gov/hazard/types.shtm> (May 8, 2006).

7. Mike Clary, "Chasing Tornadoes," *Weatherwise*, vol. 51, Jan.–Feb. 1998, p. 26.

8. "About FEMA: What We Do," *FEMA.gov*, n.d., <http://www.fema.gov/about/what.shtm> (January 23, 2006).

9. "What FEMA Doesn't Do," *FEMA.gov*, n.d., <http://www.fema.gov/library/fff02.shtm> (February 15, 2006).

10. "Worst United States Disasters," *InfoPlease.com*, n.d., <http://www.infoplease.com/ipa/A0001459.html> (January 23, 2006).

11. Ibid.

Chapter 3. Careers on the Front Lines of Emergency Management

1. "Then and Now: Brian Espe," *CNN*, June 19, 2005, <http://www.cnn.com/2005/US/04/18/cnn25.tan.espe/> (January 23, 2006).

2. Ibid.

3. "US&R Past Deployments," *FEMA.gov*, n.d., <http://www.fema.gov/usr/about5.shtm> (January 23, 2006).

4. Ibid.

5. "What You Didn't Know about Urban Search and Rescue," *FEMA.gov*, n.d., <http://www.fema.gov/usr/about1.shtm> (January 25, 2006).

6. "US&R Documents," *FEMA.gov*, n.d., <http://www.fema.gov/usr/usrdocs.shtm> (January 23, 2006).

7. "What You Didn't Know about Urban Search and Rescue."

8. "Canine's Role in Urban Search and Rescue," *FEMA.gov*, n.d., <http://www.fema.gov/about/mediacanine.shtm> (January 25, 2006).

9. "How to become an Emergency Medical Technician," *eHow.com*, n.d., <http://www.ehow.com/how_15156_become-emergency-medical.html> (January 25, 2006).

10. L. Fleming Fallon Jr., MD, DrPH, "Cardiopulmonary Resuscitation," *Health A-to-Z*, n.d., <http://www.healthatoz.com/healthatoz/Atoz/ency/cardiopulmonary_resuscitation_cpr.jsp> (January 25, 2006).

11. "How to Become a Firefighter," *eHow.com*, n.d., <http://www.ehow.com/how_8107_become-firefighter.html> (January 25, 2006); Andrea Walter, *Firefighter's Handbook: Basic Essentials of Firefighting*, basic edition, Clifton Park, NY: Delmar Learning, 2004, p. 4.

12. "Disaster Assistance Employees," *FEMA.gov*, n.d., <http://www.fema.gov/about/dae.shtm> (January 25, 2006).

Chapter 4. Careers Inside FEMA

1. "FEMA Mapping and Analysis Center," *FEMA.gov*, n.d., <http://www.gismaps.fema.gov/> (January 26, 2006).

Chapter 5. Preparing for Your Career

1. George W. Foresman, "Hurricane Preparedness: A National Perspective," *International Association of Emergency Managers*, May 24, 2006, <http://64.233.179.104/search?q= cache: ty3WScqaHg8J:iaem.com/documents/UnderSecretaryForesman WrittenTestimony.doc+%22the+preparedness+network%22& hl=en&gl=us&ct=clnk&cd=10&client=firefox-a> (June 5, 2006).

2. "About the Preparedness Network (PREPnet)," *U.S. Fire Administration*, n.d., <http://www.usfa.fema.gov/training/ prepnet/about_prepnet.shtm> (June 5, 2006).

3. "About Citizen Corps," *Citizen Corps*, n.d., <http://www. citizencorps.gov/about.shtm> (January 26, 2006).

4. "Programs and Partners," *Citizen Corps*, n.d., <http:// www.citizencorps.gov/programs/> (January 26, 2006).

5. "About NVFC," *National Volunteer Fire Council*, n.d., <http://www.nvfc.org> (May 8, 2006).

6. "Family Disaster Plan," *FEMA for Kids*, n.d., <http://www .fema.gov/kids/dzplan.htm> (January 26, 2006); "Preparing Makes Sense. Get Ready Now." brochure, U.S. Department of Homeland Security, Washington, D.C., p. 5.

7. "Volunteer Services," *American Red Cross*, n.d., <http:// www2.redcross.org/services/volunteer/0,1082,0_325_,00.html> (May 8, 2006).

8. "Becoming a Disaster Action Kid," *FEMA for Kids*, n.d., <http://www.fema.gov/kids/dizkid1.htm> (January 26, 2006).

9. "About the Emergency Management Institute (EMI)," *FEMA.gov*, February 23, 2005, <http://training.fema.gov/EMIWeb/aboutemi.asp> (May 8, 2006).

10. "About National Fire Academy," *U.S. Fire Administration*, December 20, 2005, <http://www.usfa.fema.gov/training/nfa/about/> (January 26, 2006).

11. "Noble Training Center," *FEMA.gov*, January 30, 2006, <http://training.fema.gov/emiweb/NTC/> (May 8, 2006).

12. "Disaster Preparedness for Pets," *Humane Society of the United States*, n.d., <http://www.hsus.org/hsus_field/hsus_disaster_center/disaster_preparedness_for_pets.html> (August 1, 2006).

building codes—Laws that cover how structures must be built to make sure they will be safe and secure for use. They include laws about where not to build (such as in a floodplain), materials to use or not to use, and how to fireproof buildings.

cache—A secure place to store supplies.

cardiopulmonary resuscitation (CPR)—A technique used to revive victims of a cardiac arrest (meaning that the heart has stopped).

certified—Given legal or institutional permission to practice a profession or procedure.

contaminated—Polluted; unclean or impure.

defibrillators—Devices used to restart the heart muscle by means of an electric shock.

deployment—The sending of people, equipment, or supplies to a place with a specific purpose in mind. FEMA deploys workers to the site of a disaster.

drought—A period of little or no rain.

emergency management—The supervision and direction of efforts to respond to and to prevent natural and man-made disasters.

evacuate—To remove people from an area where a disaster is about to occur or has occurred; the act of leaving or withdrawing from such an area.

first responders—The first people to respond to a disaster or emergency. This term refers to police officers, firefighters, rescue crews, emergency medical technicians, and paramedics. First responders travel to the place of disaster to help victims and to secure the area.

floodplain—A large section of land bordering a river and made of materials deposited during floods.

Geographic Information System (GIS)—A computerized database system with software that creates maps and tables for planning and decision-making.

infrastructure—Important and necessary parts that form the basis of a system. The infrastructure of the United States includes its transportation and communication services.

law enforcement—The part of the government that is responsible for making sure people follow rules and laws and maintaining order. This word usually refers to the police and sheriff's offices.

logistics—The planning and carrying out of a complex or large-scale operation. This includes the movements and the supplies necessary to make the operation a success. Logistics experts are part of FEMA's US&R teams.

mitigation—The act of making something milder or less severe.

paramedics—Health care workers who assist a doctor or provide medical treatment at the scene of an emergency.

radiation—The sending out of a dangerous type of energy.

reservist—A team member who is called into action when needed. FEMA's reservists lend help after a disaster but are not full-time FEMA employees. They are also called disaster assistance employees (DAEs).

resuscitate—To bring back to life or consciousness; to revive.

stabilize—To prevent something from moving or changing.

terrorists—People who use force or violence to try to overthrow a government or to disrupt a society.

tornadoes—Spinning funnels of air that form when a funnel of warm air quickly rises from the earth.

Books

Andryszewski, Trica. *Terrorism in America*. New York: Millbrook Press, 2002.

Baker, David. *The Department of Homeland Security*. Vero Beach, Fla.: Rourke, 2005.

Mark, Bonnie S., Aviva Layton, and Michael Chesworth. *I Know What to Do: A Kid's Guide to Natural Disasters*. New York: Magination, 1997.

McDaniel, Melissa. *Disaster Search Dogs*. New York: Bearport, 2005.

Watts, Claire. *Rescue*. New York: Dorling Kindersley, 2001.

Internet Addresses

FEMA Web site
<http://www.fema.gov>

FEMA Careers for Kids Web site
<http://www.fema.gov/kids/career.htm>

National Volunteer Fire Council
<http://www.nvfc.org>

National Registry of Emergency Medical Technicians
<http://www.nremt.org/about/nremt_news.asp>